CROSS-CULTURAL
COMMUNICATION
IN A
MULTICULTURAL
CHURCH

A MODEL FOR PROGRESSIVE CHANGE

LaDonna C. Osborn

Cross-Cultural Communication in a
Multicultural Church
ISBN 0-87943-120-2

OSBORN
PUBLISHERS

Published by Osborn Publishers
P.O. Box 10, Tulsa, OK 74102 USA
918-743-6231 • FAX 918-749-0339
Email: OSFO@aol.com • www.osborn.org

Canada: Box 281, Adelaide St. Post Sta., Toronto M5C 2J4
England: Box 148, Birmingham B3 2LG
              (A Registered Charity)

Contents

From the Author...4

Introduction 7

Chapter 1
Our Multicultural Society 10

Chapter 2
Choices Available to the Church
in a Multicultural Society 12

Chapter 3
Challenges of Participation Between
European and African Americans 17

Chapter 4
Proposed Model for Cross-Cultural
Communication in a Multicultural Group...................22

Chapter 5
Stage One: I See You...25

Chapter 6
Stage Two: I Accept You 27

Chapter 7
Stage Three: I Care About You 30

Chapter 8
Stage Four: I Know You..32

Chapter 9
Stage Five: I Respect You...37

Chapter 10
Stage Six: I Learn From You 39

Chapter 11
Stage Seven: I Work With You 41

Chapter 12
Advantages and Disadvantages of a
Multicultural Church 44

Chapter 13
Cautions for Multicultural Churches 48

Conclusion 52

References Cited 55

About the Author...59

From the Author...

Every pastor, church leader, and
sincere Christian is becoming aware
of the dramatic social changes that
impact the way they do church
ministry. Most communities have
already been influenced by the influx
of people of diverse ethnic groups or
from other nations. We accept this
reality as a positive trend for many
reasons, including its demand upon
us to grow beyond the comfort zones
of our own cultures and to learn how
to be the Church of Jesus Christ in a
culturally diverse society.

- Our headquarters church in Tulsa, Oklahoma – International Gospel Center (IGC) – is a multicultural church.
- I serve as bishop, or overseer, of IGC and hundreds of other churches throughout the States and other nations, and am a European American.
- Because of the international scope of the Osborn ministries we attract worshippers from many nations, who are now living in or visiting Tulsa.
- The Senior Pastor of IGC is an African American woman, Dr. Chyanna Mull Anthony.
- Our Board of Elders is comprised of both European and African American ministers.
- Over the years our leadership team has included men and women from Puerto Rico, Nigeria, Jamaica, Malaysia, Korea and of course many ethnically and geographically diverse Americans. The content of this book documents part of our own journey in learning to adapt to the needs of the people whom we are called to serve both locally and internationally.

As part of my academic preparation I was

asked to present a paper on the subject of cross-cultural communication. After reviewing my completed assignment, the professor encouraged me to publish the paper so that others in church and Christian education environments could benefit from its insights. Therefore, this book is presented as a brief study and practical guide for any pastor or Christian who desires to lead people of diverse cultures to increased participation in Christian ministry. While this mission is fraught with complications, it is nonetheless biblical and desperately needed in today's changing world.

This book includes a model for progressive change among multicultural groups in a local church through a seven-week course of Bible study. It is my prayer that these insights, ideas and suggestions will be helpful in guiding you into and through the compelling and rewarding journey of cross-cultural communication in your multicultural world.

–LaDonna C. Osborn, D.Min.

Introduction

Dramatic societal changes of twenty-first century America are impacting the Christian church in ever increasing ways. The cultural diversity of many congregations evidences one of these changes. Church leaders and Christian educators must develop a strategy for faith formation of individuals, within the context of the local church, that provides historical continuity of the Christian tradition while relating the Christian message to contemporary daily life.

Effective cross-cultural communication in a multicultural church requires a basic knowledge of the various people groups that the church is endeavoring to serve, sensitivity toward each group, genuine respect of individual uniqueness, and a theological approach to biblical interpretation that applies the Christian message to each group.

The purpose of this book is threefold. First, it will present the argument that building a multi-cultural church is consistent with the biblical revelation of God's ideal for the creation to coexist and function in harmony, and that the needs of our society can be served by a church which courageously honors the uniqueness of diversity.

Second, this book will introduce a proposed model of progressive change that can be used in the local church to gradually lead a group of participants through seven stages of individual change beginning with the recognition of diversity, to ultimately working together toward a common goal.

Third, this book will invite a realistic discussion of the practical advantages and

Notes

Books by Osborn Publishers

Believers in Action
Biblical Healing
Five Choices for Women Who Win
God's Big Picture
God's Love Plan
Healing the Sick
How to Be Born Again
If I Were A Woman
Jesus & Women: Answers to Three Big Questions
Life–Triump Over Tragedy
New Life for Women
Soulwinning
The Best of Life
The Good Life
The Gospel, According to T.L. & Daisy
The Message that Works
Power of Positive Desire
Woman Believer
Woman Without Limits
Women & Self-Esteem
You Are God's Best

Most Osborn books, audio or video cassettes are available at quantity
discounts for bulk purchases, to be used for gifts, resale, ministry
outreaches, education or other purposes.

Osborn Publishers, P.O. Box 10, Tulsa, OK 74102 USA
918-743-6231 • FAX 918-749-0339
Email: OSFO@aol.com • www.osborn.org

disadvantages inherent in a multicultural church, including some cautions for the church leader who would embark upon the challenging task of building a faith community within a multicultural church setting.

1

Our Multicultural Society

As the twenty-first century begins, the profile of American society is rapidly changing. According to a report in *Current Thoughts and Trends*, more than 25 percent of America's current population is non-Caucasian.[1] Demographic information published by *The National Conference* reports that

---

[1]The 'Top 20' Trends up to 2000 and Beyond." *Current Thoughts and Trends* October 1994:3.

25.3 percent of the population in Oklahoma is of an ethnic origin other than "non-Hispanic white."[2] In California that figure increases to 53.3 percent of the population. Authors James and Lillian Breckenridge condense the cultural diversity of the State of California into the following statement:

> The 1992 Los Angeles riots graphically demonstrated the consequences of ignoring our multicultural world. This city by itself is the home of more than 100 first-generation language groups. High birth rate and expanding immigration has boosted California's population by 26 percent over the last decade. Asians living in California have doubled since 1980; Latinos have grown by 70 percent.[3]

---

[2]*Building Bridges of Understanding: The 1993 Annual Report*, (New York: The National Conference, 1993) 45.

[3]James and Lillian Breckenridge, *What Color is Your God?: Multicultural Education in the Church* (Wheaton: Victor Books, 1995) 9.

2

Choices Available to the Church in a Multicultural Society

Recognizing diversity as a fact in the American culture challenges the church to formulate methodology that transmits the Christian faith across ethnic barriers, while respecting the uniqueness of various groups.

Consider three of the most obvious options
that are available to the church, segregation,
integration, and participation.

Historically, segregation of ethnic groups in
America has not served the best interest of society
as a whole or of specific groups individually.
Ultimately, segregation engenders division, and
division is contrary to the goal of the Christian
message. The principle of spiritual unity is included
in Jesus' prayer recorded in the Gospel of John:
"And now I am no longer in the world, but they
are in the world, and I am coming to you. Holy
Father, protect them in your name that you
have given me, so that they may be one, as we
are one."[4]

The principle of unity was advocated by the
Apostle Paul in his first letter to the Corinthians:
"Now I appeal to you, brothers and sisters, by the
name of our Lord Jesus Christ, that all of you be in
agreement and that there be no divisions among
you, but that you be united in the same mind and

---

[4]John 17:11 NRSV (New Revised Standard Version).

the same purpose."[5] While it is not the purpose of this author to present a detailed historical argument against segregation, it can be generally agreed that historical evidence supports the claim that segregation did not serve the public good in America, and the Christian scriptures suggest a higher ideal for the human creation.

Integration of the various ethnic groups into one single group is a second option available to the church. While this appears to fulfill the ideal of social unity, the historic record again testifies to the failure of this option. Integration results in the loss of individual distinction of all groups except for that of the dominant group. The dominant culture, or the majority, in America is Caucasian. As the population mix continues to change, it is important to know that the term "majority" does not refer to population numbers, but to the group holding the reins of power. In America, the majority of economic and political power is still in the hands of the Caucasian, middle class male. Author Anne Wilson Schaef refers to the American society as the

---

[5] 1 Corinthians 1:10 NRSV.

White Male System or "the reality" by which all other groups are assessed.[6] Radical or ethnic groups, other than Caucasian, are classified as "minority" regardless of their numeric strength. It is the opinion of this author that while segregation engenders division, integration results in domination of the weaker by the more powerful.

We must remember the value set forth in Christian scripture: "There is no longer Jew or Greek, there is no longer slave or free, there is no longer male and female; for all of you are one in Christ Jesus."[7] The biblical principle of equality between all people regardless of race, economic status, gender (or other distinctions) establishes a criterion by which Christian ministries must be evaluated.

The third option available to the church is participation. While segregation engenders division and integration results in domination, it is the premise of this author that participation promotes

---

[6] Anne Wilson Schaef, *Women's Reality: An Emerging Female System in a White Male Society* (San Francisco: Harper and Row, 1981) 2-3.
[7] Galatians 3:28 NRSV.

restoration. Restoration of the relationship between God and the creation is the central theme of the Christian story. While there are myriad theological views, it can generally be agreed that this restoration involves participation between God and the creation: initiative on the part of God (grace) and response on the part of human persons (faith). This principle of participation is seen throughout the biblical text, and directly stated in the Gospel of John: "For God so loved the world that he gave his only Son, so that everyone who believes in him may not perish but may have eternal life."[8]

When considering the options available to the church in a multicultural society, we must remember the example of Jesus' ministry that also occurred in a cross-cultural setting.[9] His example suggests that the church today needs to develop cross-cultural communication and participation skills.

---

[8]John 3.16 NRSV.

[9]Two examples of Jesus relating across cultural barriers are recorded in Mark 7:24-30 (the Syrophoenician woman), and in John 4:4-39 (the Samaritan woman). In both instances, he acted contrary to societal norms in order to reveal God and to model the ideal behavior of one living in relationship with God.

3

Challenges of Participation between European and African Americans

While there are many types of diversity among people, such as life-setting pluralities, religious pluralism, etc., it best serves the specific purpose of this presentation to focus on participation between European and

African Americans in the Christian church setting. As David Hesselgrave has stated, "It is well to keep in mind that effective communication is not easily achieved and miscommunication is not easy to avoid."[10] While racial tensions exist among many groups, there are historic factors that complicate the relationship between Whites and Blacks in America. The attitudes and practices that promote fruitful cross-cultural communication and faith formation in Black/White multicultural groups will also produce positive results among groups of other ethnic backgrounds. [11]

We will consider three challenges of multi-cultural participation between European and African Americans. First, each group has a different history. For example, while European *Americans* relate to their history (the discovery of the Americas; the conquering of the "wild" west; and the freedoms claimed by the Constitution and the

---

[10]David J. Hesselgrave, *Communicating Christ Cross-Culturally*, 2nd ed. (Grand Rapids: Zondervan Publishing House, 1991) 46.
[11]Carley H. Dodd, *Dynamics of Intercultural Communication*, 4th ed. (Madison: Brown and Benchmark, 1995) 65.

Bill of Rights) with a sense of pride, African *Americans* remember their history (the stolen heritage of their ancient roots and their forced immigration under the slave master's chain) with a dual sense of shame and resentment. Cross-cultural communication in a multicultural church group of European and African Americans must consider their different histories.

Second, each group has dangerous memories. For example, African Americans may remember the deception of the slave owners whose decisions were usually motivated by self-interest, and ask, "Why should I trust the words of Whites?" African Americans may remember that the Christian scriptures were interpreted to justify slavery, and ask "How can I have faith in the God of that book?" Fortunately, as documented by author Katie Cannon, "The Black religious experience equipped slaves with a biblical under-standing that called them to engage in acts of rebellion for freedom. The faith assertions of the Black church encouraged slaves to reject any teachings that attempted to reconcile slavery with the gospel of Jesus Christ."[12] Black Theology has surfaced to reinterpret the image of the "white Jesus" into a vital image for their liberation from White oppression.[13] African Americans may remember the stories of uncles, fathers, grand-fathers, and brothers lynched without legal recourse, and ask, "How can I believe in the systems created by the Whites?" European Americans, on the other hand, may remember the stories of dangerous black men. How do they overcome the fear? European Americans remember that their ancestors were brutal toward other human beings. How can they forget the shame? Cross-cultural communication in a multicultural group of European and African Americans must consider their dangerous and diverse memories.

Third, each group is affected by distorted progress. Since the Civil Rights Movement in the

---

[12]Katie Geneva Cannon, "The Emergence of Black Feminist Consciousness," *Feminist Interpretation of the Bible,* ed. Letty M. Russell (Philadelphia: Westminster Press: 1985) 31.

[13]James H. Cone, *A Black Theology of Liberation* (Maryknoll: Orbis, 1986) 110-111.

1960s many Americans have wanted to believe that we have made progress toward overcoming racism. However, as stated earlier, the majority of the power is still in the hands of European Americans; there is social courtesy between the races but too few personal relationships exist across cultural lines; and while there is a surface appearance of social concern, personal biases and stereotypical assumptions remain intact. Cross-cultural communication in a multicultural church group of European and African Americans must consider the distorted perception of progress within society.

4

Proposed Model for Cross-Cultural Communication in a Multicultural Church Group

In order to effect Christian education in a multicultural church, cross-cultural communication must occur between individuals of diverse ethnic groups. A church is to be a community of individuals bonded by a common faith and working together as a redemptive agent in society. Since American society is diverse, it seems logical for the members of a multicultural church to address the issues of ethnic difference and to live and work together toward common goals. For this to occur, people of differing views must gradually change in order to develop relationships with each other.[14] It is the view of this author that healthy and lasting change within a local church must occur gradually. If change is rushed, people may feel threatened and choose to leave the church. This defeats the purpose of the church.

The model presented here for cross-cultural communication for the purpose of faith formation in a multi-cultural church is a model of progressive change. This model follows seven stages of learning that begin with the recognition of diversity (I see you) and end with participation toward a common goal (I work with you).

---

[14]The word *change* is used to convey the process of individual transformation through increased knowledge and understanding, resulting in progress toward the fulfillment of human potential.

This model of progressive change is recommended as a seven-week Bible study class comprised of adults from various ethnic and cultural backgrounds. Each week includes a class objective, a Bible text or exercise, and student participation.

5

Stage One:
I See You

The objective of the first week is to
recognize differences among the
members of the class. The atmosphere
of the class is to be one of openness
and honesty. It is important that the
uniqueness of each student be
appreciated. The facilitators should
affirm cultural differences and
encourage the students to participate
in discussions from their individual
cultural perspective.

Often people try to suppress their differences in an attempt to avoid discomfort or conflict. The result is unresolved tensions in the church that cause more problems than dealing with specific issues openly.[15] It would be helpful if the facilitators of the class were from at least two different cultural groups.

The Bible exercise for Stage One can be to have the students identify diverse types of Bible characters who had a relationship with God. For example, according to the biblical text, eunuchs, shepherds, children, sisters, brothers, fishermen, Israelites, Samaritans, Canaanites, Cyrenians, Egyptians, a divorced woman, and persons of various professions and social classes had faith relationships with God and were significant in human history. The class will have been successful if the students begin to SEE diversity.

---

[15]Stephen Kliewer, *How to Live with Diversity in the Local Church* (New York: Albans Institute, 1987) 27.

6

Stage Two: I Accept You

The objective of the second week is to help the students not only to see differences, but also to accept them without feeling personally compromised or devalued. The economic system of America places an ascending or descending value on everything, including people. Following is a sociologist's assessment:

> The United States is a mosaic of different social groups and categories. However, these groups are not equal in power, resources, prestige, or presumed worth. They are differentially ranked on each of these dimensions. But why is one group alleged to be superior to another? The basic reason is differential power — power derived from superior numbers, technology, weapons, property, or economic resources. The people holding superior power in a society establish a system of inequality by dominating less powerful groups, and this system of inequality is then maintained and perpetuated by power.[16]

Society tends to grade "difference," rather than to simply accept and affirm it. According to Carley Dodd, "We should look upon differences

---

[16] D. Stanley Eitzen and Maxine Baca Zinn, *Social Problems* (Boston: Allyn and Bacon, 1994) 191-192.

as an opportunity, a resource from which to learn exciting things about a new culture, a new person, and ourselves."[17] The emphasis of Stage Two is on the importance of accepting diversity as a wonderful fact of life.

The biblical lesson can focus on the conflict between Miriam, the sister of Moses, and the Cushite woman whom he married.[18] The class discussion could center on the possible cultural reasons why Miriam (of Middle Eastern heritage) had difficulty accepting the Cushite woman (of African heritage) into the family. The class will have been successful if the students begin to ACCEPT the fact of diversity.

---

[17]Dodd 93.
[18]Numbers 12.

7

Stage Three: I Care About You

The objective of the third week is to progress beyond seeing and accepting diversity to begin caring about people of different cultures. One way to encourage genuine caring between people is for them to share an emotional experience. For example, this would be an opportunity for students to share stories with the group about personal experiences of prejudice. By Stage Three some

bonding is beginning to occur among the participants and they are ready for the deeper emotional
involvement that accompanies caring about
someone of another culture.

The Bible lesson for Stage Three can deal with
Jesus' encounter with the woman of Samaria.[19] Class
facilitators can lead the students in a discussion of
the various ways that Jesus demonstrated care for
the woman. For example, Jesus cared about her
family, about her reputation, about her faith views,
and about her knowledge of Himself as Messiah.
This discussion teaches the students how to relate
to and communicate with a person from a different
background, with differing views. The class will have
been successful if the students begin to genuinely
CARE about someone of another culture.

---

[19]John 4.

8

Stage Four:
I Know You

The objective of the fourth week is
to develop the sense of knowing
from the perspective of a person of
another culture or group. This can
only happen after a person has seen
diversity, has accepted diversity, and
has begun to care about someone
who is different from them. By this
stage in progressive change, the
class members can discuss specific
differences that make up who they

are as cultural people groups. For example, an interesting discussion between European and African American women is their differing attitudes about men and the historic and cultural reasons for the difference. A study of African heritage reveals significant information:

> In most West African tribes, women were persons in their own right, with responsibilities and privileges not always based on their husbands' and fathers' patriarchal powers. Women controlled marketplaces, and their economic monopoly provided them with leverage for autonomous activity and with opportunities for leadership experiences.[20]

In a society that does not allow the African American man to compete freely in the economic market, he will continue to be driven from the home where he feels useless, unable to adequately

---

[20]Rosemary Radford Ruether and Rosemary Skinner, eds., *Women and Religion in America Vol. 2: The Colonial and Revolutionary Periods* (San Francisco: Harper and Row, 1983) 233.

support his family, and the Black woman will continue doing whatever is necessary to hold the family together. While the Black family is often misunderstood and even judged as pathological, a deeper insight results in a profound respect for the strength and values of the Black woman who teaches her children to survive within a society that institutionalizes racial hatred.[21]

Psychologist David Augsburger confirms at least four levels of cross-cultural awareness: 1) awareness of superficial cultural traits; 2) awareness of significant and subtle cultural traits that contrast with one's own; 3) awareness of the meanings of cultural traits that contrast sharply with one's own; and 4) awareness of how another culture feels from the standpoint of the insider. [22] The more one knows about another person's culture, the greater the chance of open dialogue across cultural lines.

---

[21]Elizabeth A. Peterson, *African American Women: A Study of Will and Success* (Jefferson, NC: McFarland, 1956) 66.
[22]David W. Augsburger, *Pastoral Counseling Across Cultures* (Philadelphia: Westminster Press, 1986) 26.

Stage Four: I Know You

The Bible exercise for Stage Four can be a
discussion of Sarah and Hagar.[23] Historically, in
the Christian church, European American women
have related to the character of Sarah, while
African American women have related to the
slave, Hagar. One writer associates Hagar
as follows:

> As a symbol of the oppressed, Hagar
> becomes many things to many people.
> Most especially, all sorts of rejected
> women find their stories in her. She is
> the faithful maid exploited, the black
> woman used by the male and abused
> by the female of the ruling class, the
> surrogate mother, the resident alien
> without legal recourse. . .[24]

The emphasis of this week's discussion is:
"Because I know you, I see this story differently."
James Cone, one of the foremost proponents of
Black Theology, states:

---

[23]Genesis 21.
[24]Phyllis Trible, *Texts of Terror: Literary-Feminist Readings of Biblical
Narratives* (Philadelphia: Fortress Press, 1984) 28.

> No one can respond to God outside
> of his or her existential context. . .
> although we know God as individuals
> all theology is influenced by and
> reflects — in one way or another —
> the historical and experiential circum-
> stances of a people, a nation, or a
> neighborhood. God comes to us and
> we respond to God where we are
> placed in the world.[25]

This suggests that each person's view of and
relationship with God is valid. It is important for
the students to be able to discuss how Hagar and
Sarah may have felt, leading them to the conclusion
that knowing more about the backgrounds of each
woman increases the impact and application of
scripture in their lives. The class will have been
successful if students begin to KNOW the value of
another person's view.

---

[25]James H. Cone and Gayraud S. Wilmore, *Black Theology: A Documentary History Vol. 2: 1980-1992* (Maryknoll: Orbis, 1983) 165.

9

Stage Five:
I Respect You

The objective of the fifth week is
to allow the students to recognize
and celebrate their progressive
change toward positive Christian
relationships with people of different
backgrounds. When difference is
seen, there can be acceptance.
Following acceptance is genuine
caring. Caring leads to a deepened
knowledge of another person's point
of view. Knowledge is followed by

honest respect. At the fifth stage of progressive change, students can enjoy observing how their views have changed and expanded to include the attitudes of others.

The Bible lesson for Stage Five can be on the vision that Peter (a Jew) had of something like a sheet coming down from heaven containing all types of unclean animals.[26] Peter's attitude toward Gentiles (considered "unclean" by Jews) was changed by this supernatural experience, when the voice said to him, "What God has made clean, you must not call profane."[27] Discussing the change in Peter allows the students to recognize changes in their own attitudes as they have grown spiritually, more able to see other people from God's perspective. The class will be successful if the students recognize that they are indeed learning to RESPECT and value the uniqueness of others.

---

[26]Acts 10.
[27]Acts 10:15 NRSV.

10

Stage Six:
I Learn
From You

The objective of the sixth week is
to allow the students to learn from
one another. Progressive change is
evident when people begin to learn
from those of a different cultural or
ethnic group. This indicates that old
biases are being laid aside for the
sake of a greater common good.

The Bible lesson for this week

can be a study of Moses and Jethro and how they learned from one another. An interesting exercise would be to team up members of the class (intentionally from diverse groups) and have them search the biblical record and discover together the numerous things that Moses learned from Jethro, a man of a different culture than Moses. The class will be successful if the students indeed LEARN from someone of another culture.

11

Stage Seven: I Work With You

The objective of the seventh week is the ultimate goal of the class. The model of progressive change results in people from different cultures working together toward a common goal. The group is ready to agree upon a specific task and work together to accomplish something for greater society. Class members' individual progress equips them to accomplish something on behalf of others that may not have been possible prior to this seven-week experience. It is appropriate to plan public recognition of the class, in the local church, and to highlight the cross-cultural nature of the activity that they accomplish together.

The Bible lesson for this week could be based on the New Testament church of Antioch. The church leaders comprised "Barnabas, Simeon who was called Niger, Lucius of Cyrene, Manaen a member of the court of Herod the ruler, and Saul."[28] Upon investigation, the students will observe that the leadership team in Antioch was comprised of two Jews, two Blacks, and one Greek. It is the goal of Christians in the church to be able to work together with a common vision and a common faith regardless of cultural or racial differences. The class will be successful if the students have learned to WORK together toward a defined goal.

---

[28] Acts 13:1 NRSV.

In this model of progressive change, students have been gradually introduced to factors of diversity, persons of diversity, and biblical support of diversity within an atmosphere of acceptance and purpose. Students have experienced positive personal change that has evolved from the first stage of SEEING diversity to the ultimate stage of WORKING together toward a common objective. As Christians in a diverse society, participation across cultural boundaries is necessary if the church is to accomplish its redemptive mission in the world. That mission, for contemporary theologians is "the deepening of the love of God and humanity. . . .focus[ing] on the plight of the oppressed and the need for total human liberation. . . . Racial and sexual discrimination should be abolished in every church as each individual life is brought under the discipline of sacrificial love."[29]

---

[29]Deane William Ferm, *Contemporary American Theologies: A Critical Survey* (San Francisco: Harper and Row, 1981) 152-153.

12

Advantages and Disadvantages of a Multicultural Church

While the goal of participation among people groups within a multicultural church is an ideal, it must also be understood that there are disadvantages as well as advantages to a culturally diverse congregation. One disadvantage of a multicultural

church is the tendency toward diminished interaction among the members. While people from
different cultures may be able to worship together,
there may not be a desire for social interaction
between people of diverse groups. Relationships
are vital to the health and growth of a local
church; therefore, this lack of (or delayed)
interaction can be a hindrance.

Another possible disadvantage of a multicultural church is the reduced visual appeal of the
congregation. Americans are socialized to see
homogenous groups as more attractive than groups
that include diversity. Therefore, a congregation
may appear to be an odd assortment of people,
or less attractive, based on their various colors,
shapes, mannerisms, clothing tastes, etc.

A third disadvantage of a multicultural church
(similar to the first) is the potential difficulty in
assimilating new members into its various
activities. It is often easier to absorb new members
into relationships and volunteer programs with

people who are similar to them.

Another obvious disadvantage of a multi-cultural church is the risk of minority groups losing their distinction by being swallowed up in the majority culture of the church. A final disadvantage of a multicultural church is that leaders expend much physical energy teaching people to work together as one corporate body.

In spite of the numerous disadvantages of a multicultural church, there are the important advantages. For example, diversity in the church encourages tolerance among the people. This is a Christ-like characteristic that is necessary for involvement by the church in the greater community. Also, diversity facilitates more creative dialogue that is critical in this pluralistic society. Diversity in the church leads to increased effectiveness in society, and meaningful personal growth in the members who are involved[30] Jack Seymour presents one of the foremost arguments in favor of the multicultural church:

---

[30]Kliewer 10-14.

> The universality of the [Christian]
> message calls for enculturation to be
> part of the process. Moreover, we
> always receive the gospel from some-
> one else, rather than through an inner
> experience directly from God. . . . The
> mediation of the message of Jesus
> across the centuries and the oceans,
> from hand to hand, is a constituent
> part of that message itself. . .[31]

Remembering that the church is God's
redemptive agent in the world, following the
example of Jesus' ministry on earth, the
advantages of building a multicultural church
far outweigh the disadvantages.

---

[31]Sawickii, Marianne, "Tradition and Sacamental Education," in *Theological Approaches to Christian Education*, eds. Jack L. Seymour and Donald E. Miller (Nashville: Abingdon, 1990) 45.

13

Cautions for Multicultural Churches

For the church leader who is considering building a multicultural church, there are at least five significant cautions if cross-cultural communication for the purpose of faith formation in this setting is to be effective. First, avoid the notion that time will cure the problems of racism or cultural difference. The multicultural congregation must actively work together toward social justice. Teaching models, such as the above-suggested model of progressive change, will help the congregants to face their fears and will lead them toward an attitude and lifestyle of cooperative interaction with those of different backgrounds.

Second, church leaders and educators must revise all curriculum and teaching materials to replace ethnocentrism[32] with an awareness of diversity. Curriculum is often designed for homogenous church groups. An article published in the *Religious Education* journal emphasizes this fact:

> Church curricula for children from
> the 1920s to the 1960s depicted Jesus
> with northern European features such
> as light-colored hair. Children of
> Anglo-Saxon descent were to help
> other European immigrants assimilate

---

[32]Ethnocentrism is an evaluation of one's culture as better than or superior to another culture. (Dodd 69)

and become good Americans. But nonwhites were unable to melt into American society and were thus seen as outsiders. These facts reflected the implicit assimilationist and racist ideology of curriculum writers.[33]

While the religious curriculum writers have made progress, individual teachers must become more sensitive to the subtle messages being promoted, and make changes where necessary.

Third, pastors and teachers must be alert to avoid passing on the vision of the dominant culture to the children and youth. Sociologists and educators warn, "Studies continue to demonstrate that young children, as early as three years of age, are aware of ethnic differences."[34] It is easy to dialogue on one level while modeling outdated values on another level. The minds of children and youth absorb the subtle messages displayed

---

[33]Russel G. Moy, "Biculturalism, Race, and the Bible," *Religious Education* 88 (1993):423.

[34]Edith W. King, Marilyn Chipman and Marta Cruz-Janzen, *Educating Young Children in a Diverse Society* (Boston: Ally and Bacon, 1994) 15.

thorough adult behavior more quickly than they
absorb the words of idealistic lectures.

Fourth, it is important to develop a multicultural style in the worship services (such as in
varieties of music) and to affirm diversity in social
activities. As stated by Jack Seymour, "The task
of the church is to get up-to-date. We are an
evolutionary people, not static. We must live
historically by participating in the events that
shape the future."[35]

Fifth, leaders of multicultural churches must
share their power with those of other ethnic groups
who represent the people in their congregations.
All of the other considerations will be worth little
if the authority in the church remains in the hands
of the dominant culture. It is the opinion of this
author that shared leadership is critical to the
success of cross-cultural communication and
faith formation in the multicultural church.

---

[35]O'Gorman, Robert T., "Latin American Theology and Education,"
in *Theological Approaches to Christian Education*, eds. Jack L. Seymour
and Donald E. Miller (Nashville: Abingdon, 1990) 195.

Conclusion

Recognizing the diversity of American society is the beginning of planned evolution toward a multicultural church that more fully reflects society as a whole. Having tried segregation and integration without success, it is time to try participation among people of different histories for the purpose of restoring our society. Secular education is accepting the ideal of participation among various groups. For example, educators are using the

Conclusion

term "multicultural education" to define a teaching strategy that promotes the strength and value of diversity; promotes human rights and respect for all people; promotes social justice and equal opportunity; and promotes equality in the distribution of power among groups.[36] How much more, the church should come together in the spirit of unity, equipping Christians of all backgrounds to value one another and work together as God's redemptive agent in the world.

Churches can encourage the ideal of participation if they will embark upon a faith strategy that leads people into new ways of thinking about diversity, such as suggested in the model of progressive change. This model is based on seven stages of change formation beginning with awareness and leading to cooperative action, I see you; I accept you; I care about you; I know you; I respect you; I learn from you; and I work with you. While the task of cross-cultural

---

[36]Christine E. Sleeter and Carl A. Grant, *Making Choices for Multicultural Education: Five Approaches to Race, Class, and Gender* (New York: Macmillan, 1988) 138-139.

communication for the purpose of faith formation in a multicultural church is complex, it is the option consistent with the needs of our society and with the overall redemptive mission of the Christian church.

References Cited

Augsburger, David W. Pastoral *Counseling Across Cultures*. Philadelphia: Westminster, 1986.

Breckenridge, James, and Lillian Breckenridge. *What Color is Your God: Multicultural Education in the Church*. Wheaton: Victor Books, 1995.

Building Bridges of Understanding: The 1993 Annual Report. New York: The National Conference, 1993.

Cannon, Katie Geneva. "The Emergence of Black Feminist Consciousness." *Feminist Interpretation of the Bible*. Ed. Letty M. Russell. Philadelphia: Westminster Press, 1985. 30-40.

Cross-Cultural Communication

Carter, Harold A., Wyatt Tee Walker, and William A., Jones, Jr. *The African American Church.* New York: Martin Luther King Fellows Press, 1991.

Cone, James H. *A Black Theology of Liberation.* Maryknoll: Orbis, 1986.

Cone, James H., and Gayraud S. Wilmore. *Black Theology: A Documentary History Vol. 2: 1980-1992.* Maryknoll: Orbis, 1993.

Dodd, Carley H. *Dynamics of Intercultural Communication.* 4th ed. Madison: Brown and Benchmark, 1995.

Eitzen, D. Stanley, and Maxine Baca Zinn. *Social Problems.* Boston: Allyn and Bacon, 1994.

Ferm, Deane William. *Contemporary American Theologies: A Critical Survey.* San Francisco: Harper and Row, 1981.

Hesselgrave, David J. *Communicating Christ Cross-Cuturally.* Grand Rapids: Zondervan Publishing House, 1991.

King, Edith W., Marilyn Chipman, and Marta

56

Cruz-Janzen. *Educating Young Children in a Diverse Society.* Boston: Allyn and Bacon, 1994.

Kliewer, Stephen. *How to Live with Diversity in the Local Church.* New York: The Albany Institute, 1987.

Moy, Russell G. "Biculturalism, Race, and the Bible." *Religious Education* 88 (1993): 415-433.

Peterson, Elizabeth A. *African American Women: A Study of Will and Success.* Jefferson, NC: McFarland, 1992.

Ruether, Rosemary Radford, and Rosemary Skinner Keller, eds. *Women and Religion in America Vol. 2: The Colonial and Revolutionary Periods.* San Francisco: Harper and Row, 1983.

Schaef, Anne Wilson. *Women's Reality: An Emerging Female System in a White Male Society.* San Francisco: Harper and Row, 1981.

Seymour, Jack L., and Donald E. Miller. *Theological Approaches to Christian Education.* Nashville: Abingdon, 1990.

Sleeter, Christine E., and Carl A. Grant. *Making*

Choices for Multicultural Education: Five Approaches to Race, Class, and Gender. New York: Macmillan, 1988.

"The 'Top 20' Trends up to 2000 and Beyond." *Current Thoughts and Trends* Oct. 1994:3.

Trible, Phyllis. *Texts of Terror: Literary Feminist Readings of Biblical Narratives.* Philadelphia: Fortress Press, 1984.

ABOUT THE AUTHOR

LaDonna C. Osborn, D.Min.

LaDonna Osborn is Founder and
Bishop of *International Gospel Center
Churches and Ministries* (IGCFCM),
with its headquarters church in Tulsa,
Oklahoma. She is the Vice President
and CEO of *Osborn International*
(also known as OSFO International),
the world missionary organization

founded by her parents in 1949. She is also a member of the College of Bishops for the *International Communion of Charismatic Churches* (ICCC), representing over 10 million believers on every continent. Dr. Osborn's national and international travel and ministry schedule includes pastors' and leadership training conferences, women's and mission's conferences, Bible School and Seminary lectures and mass miracle evangelism crusades. Her Bible courses and books are distributed to national church leaders in countries around the world.

Dr. Osborn's articulate expression and demonstration of the Gospel – from a broad worldview – teaches and energizes faith in and dedication to the Church's ministry of reconciliation. She sets a positive and inspiring example for both women and men in all areas of church ministry and Christian leadership.

LaDonna Osborn earned a Bachelor of Arts (BA) Degree from Oklahoma City University, a Master of Arts (MA) Degree in Practical Theology from Oral Roberts University, and a Doctor of Ministry (D.Min.) Degree from American Christian College and Seminary. She was awarded the honorary Doctor of Divinity Degree (DD) from both Bethel Christian College and Zoe University, and the Doctor of Humane Letters Degree (HLD) from the Wesley Synod. She is listed in *Who's Who Among Students in American Universities and Colleges; Who's Who in the South and Southwest; Who's Who of Emerging Leaders in America; Who's Who in America; Who's Who of American Woman, Who's Who in Religion,* and the *World Who's Who of Women.*

Notes